Animals

Bear

Bird

Camel

Cat

Chameleon

Cheetah

Chicken

Cow

Crocodile

Deer

Dog

Dolphin

Donkey

Eagle

Elephant

Fish

Flamingo

Fox

Frog

Giraffe

Goat

Goose

Gorilla

Heyna

Hippopotamus

Horse

Kangaroo

Leopard

Lion

Meerkat

Monkey

Ostrich

Owl

Parrot

Peacock

Penguin

Pig

Pigeon

Rabbit

Rat

Rhino

Sheep

Snake

Squirrel

Tiger

Tortoise

Vulture

Whale

Zebra

www.ingramcontent.com/pod-product-compliance
Lightning Source LLC
Chambersburg PA
CBHW041520070526
44585CB00002B/26